The
Anniversary
Book

Illustrated symbols & themes of love,
year by year

STEVE PALIN

Merlin Unwin Books

First published in Great Britain
by Merlin Unwin Books Ltd 2020

Merlin Unwin Books Ltd
Palmers House
Ludlow
Shropshire SY8 1DB
UK

www.merlinunwin.co.uk

ISBN 978-1-913159-18-4

Typeset in 12 point Minion Pro by Merlin Unwin
Printed by 1010 Printing International Ltd

For Cathy, Michael & Samantha,
Mickey & Louis
with love

Introduction

The celebration of wedding anniversaries can take many forms, but often includes the giving of gifts. Indeed, the word 'wedlock' derives from the Old English 'wedlac'; its meanings include making a pledge, offering a gift, or perhaps endorsing the pledge with a gift.

Having said that, the giving of gifts to celebrate the anniversary of a wedding appears to have been a relatively recent development. It had been a German tradition since the 18th century to celebrate 25 and 50 years of marriage with a silver and gold wreath respectively. However, it was not a practice shared with the English-speaking world.

Until the last 150 years, the concept of marrying for love wasn't widespread; arranged marriages were the norm. These unions were seen as ways to cement relationships between two families, for social or financial benefit.

But although love-matches gained ground in Victorian England, it was still a common belief that this sort of betrothal was much more likely to fail. To prevent this, gifts were given both as a reward for success as well as an incentive to carry on the good work! Prince Albert, influenced by the German tradition, particularly encouraged the giving of such anniversary presents.

Consequently, from the mid nineteenth century, various publications began to include lists of gifts associated with specific anniversaries. They started modestly: 1st, 5th, 10th, 25th, 50th and 75th, but gradually expanded over time and started to include gemstones and flowers, refining a tradition of attaching meaning to both which had begun thousands of years before. Retailers began to recognise a potential new market opportunity. In 1937 the American National Retail Jewelers

Association published a much-extended list which defined appropriate gifts for each year up to 25, then for each subsequent five-year interval after that. This formed the basis of many lists in current circulation and indeed reflects the sequence of illustrations in this book.

However, although this and the more recent Chicago Public Library's 'modern list' are often quoted as authoritative sources, the truth is that there is no single definitive list. One can find any number of traditional UK lists, modern or contemporary British lists and separate American lists but there are many different versions. Examine ten lists and you might get ten different interpretations of the symbolism of a gemstone, ten different associations of a flower, ten different meanings of the theme or ten different attributes for its history.

The most modern lists concerning flowers and gemstones are perhaps the most inconsistent and varied. There are contradictions, overlaps, omissions or inventions. With the advent of the internet particularly (one website invites readers to suggest their own 'internet-age gifts'), one could despair of deciding which lists have integrity and which are fanciful.

This compilation has taken those elements which are either the longest-standing or the ones with the most numerous references, commonality or consistency across the various list sources. Ultimately, they are all just a bit of fun, but it is hoped that this book will bring some of the many variations together to offer a greater insight into the associations and help any buyer purchase a suitable gift for the occasion.

Steve Palin

First Anniversary

֍ **The traditional gift is paper**
֍ **The modern gift is a clock**

Think not because you are now wed, that all your courtship's at an end
– Antonio Hurtado de Mendoza, Spanish dramatist 1586-1644

When anniversary lists were just starting out in the mid nineteenth century, the first wedding milestone was actually identified in one publication as **sugar**, but this was for only the first month of being a couple, not a full year. One hopes that most marriages were able to survive at least that long!

The fragility and ephemeral nature of **paper** reflects the delicacy of a new relationship. Anniversary themes generally become more representative of strength, resilience and value as they progress down the years.

Clocks have an obvious association with the idea of passing time together, but watches in particular are the theme for the 15th anniversary – watch out for that!

Flowers have long been associated with romance and there exists a whole symbolic language of flowers, called floriography. Some of this goes back to ancient times but like many sentimental issues, floriography was popularised in the Victorian era, with such novelties as 'talking bouquets'. **Carnations** are most often associated with the first anniversary. Different coloured carnations are said to represent different things, but red ones symbolise admiration, love and affection, and pink ones gratitude. It may not be a good idea to send yellow carnations, which reflect disappointment or rejection!

Gemstones have many associations with birth, myths and legends. Both **freshwater pearl** and **mother of pearl** feature commonly for the first anniversary, but **gold** and **peridot** also get a mention in some lists. Freshwater pearls are said to encourage purity of body and mind.

Second Anniversary

ℬ **Cotton is the traditional theme**
ℬ **China is the modern equivalent**

An infinity of passion can be contained in one minute, like a crowd in a small space – Gustave Flaubert, *Madame Bovary*

Cotton can signify prosperity, wealth and well-being, but also strength and adaptability, qualities for a successful partnership. A natural material made from the fluffy fibres of the cotton plant, cotton is both soft and strong. Thinking of a gift made from cotton should pose no major problems for those wishing to buy, but there are some original ideas out there. You can now even get various items of jewellery made from cotton, or a cotton-scented candle. Or how about some cotton grass for a pot or garden?

The modern theme is a gift of **china**, which got its name from the country of the same name which first produced white porcelain. Subsequently, all other glazed ceramic imitations became known as china.

There are various options in the flowers which are identified for second anniversaries. Many lists suggest **cosmos**, the 'love flower', while others include **lily of the valley**, signifying purity. Of course, depending on when the couple got married, it may not always be easy or convenient to source the appropriate blooms, though photographs or pictures of the right flowers offer an alternative out of season.

There is also a choice for the second anniversary's associated gemstone. By far the most often referred to is the **garnet**, especially red garnet, but **rose quartz** also features in a number of lists. Garnet is variously described as representing physical strength, endurance, prosperity, abundance, gratitude, service, and safety when travelling.

Third Anniversary

❧ The traditional theme is leather
❧ The modern theme is crystal or glass

I ask you to pass through life at my side – to be my second self, and best earthly companion – Charlotte Brontë, English novelist 1816-1855

Leather is strong and durable, just as a successful relationship should be. It has been associated throughout history with power and protection, used as parts of armour, boots, headwear and saddles etc. There is also a dimension of elegance and luxury in leather, and there is great choice across a wide price range for a gift – thank goodness you haven't reached the diamond celebrations yet! But note that an alternative modern theme for the ninth anniversary is also leather.

Two further materials are widely recognised as modern third anniversary equivalents: **crystal** and **glass**. Crystal symbolises purity and perfection. Whilst crystal can relate to many different types of stones, it usually refers to rock crystal or clear quartz. Glass can have contradictory associations – both fragility as well as protection. But a lead-crystal glass gift would seem to kill two birds with one stone. Crystal is also the primary gift for the 15th anniversary.

Fuchsia is generally the flower associated with the third anniversary. With its extravagant-looking flowerhead, the plant symbolises abundance, but fuchsias with bright red flowers especially indicate confiding love: very appropriate for a wedding anniversary.

There are three main gemstones which appear across different anniversary lists. The most common seems to be **crystal**, but **jade** and **pearl** are also mentioned in numerous lists and both are symbolic of purity, resonating with that of crystal.

Fourth Anniversary

The traditional theme is fruit & flowers; linen or silk
The modern equivalent gifts are appliances

Grow old with me, the best is yet to be
– Robert Browning, English poet 1812-1889

Any flowers are acceptable for the fourth anniversary, but many lists specify **geraniums**. Some wild varieties are called cranesbills because the seed-heads look like the bill of a crane. There are as many interpretations of the geranium's symbolism as there are types and varieties of the flower. They can be associated with ingenuity and friendship; red ones are, unsurprisingly, associated with passion and love (they can be an ingredient in love potions – so get your pestle and mortar out!) and white ones with innocence and purity. But geraniums can also be associated with melancholy, sadness, foolishness and stupidity. You might be better to give a box of chocolates.

Fruit represents the ongoing cycle of life, with its seeds hidden within, while **linen** is regarded as a symbol of purity and was the fabric of choice for holy priests. **Silk** is the main theme for the 12th anniversary and is discussed in more detail there.

Both **amethyst** and **blue topaz** gemstones are listed for the fourth anniversary. However, because the colour associated with the occasion is blue, the blue topaz seems to be gain preference. The blue topaz represents love, romance and loyalty.

Fifth Anniversary

🌿 **Wood is the traditional theme**
🌿 **Silver is the modern equivalent**

Fight less, cuddle more. Demand less, serve more. Text less, talk more. Criticise less, compliment more – Dave Willis, Christian pastor 1978-

Wood symbolises strength, integrity, and from certain long-lived trees, longevity. There are limitless artefacts made of wood, or you might even want to gift a tree itself, or perhaps a subscription to a woodland or environmental organisation. Wood is the traditional theme for the fifth, but also the modern theme for the sixth anniversary.

There is also plenty of gift choice if you decide on the **silverware** theme including cutlery and other tableware made of either real silver or materials resembling silver.

The flower associated with the fifth anniversary is the humble **daisy**, of which there are many different types including the **gerbera**. The daisy was the sacred flower of Freya, Norse goddess of love, beauty, and fertility.

Different lists identify a number of fifth anniversary gemstones, including **sapphire** (see 45th) **pink tourmaline** (see 17th) and the illustrated **turquoise**. Like many opaque gemstones, the latter's potential to be imitated and artificially altered has lowered its commercial value somewhat, but don't let that put you off giving it as a gift – it is considered to have healing and protective qualities and gives the wearer courage. It is also said to bring luck, friendship and love.

Sixth Anniversary

⊛ **The traditional theme in the UK is sugar and in the US iron**
⊛ **Wood is the modern equivalent**

Love means never having to say you're sorry – Erich Segal, *Love Story*

Before more comprehensive anniversary lists were established, **sugar** was the gift for just the first month. But now it's six years, so push the boat out – thrill the happy couple and buy them another bag of sugar!

Sugar (or candy) is sometimes also listed for the traditional US theme, but more commonly the gift for the fifth anniversary is iron, symbolising strength and fortitude as the couple progress through their years together. The alternative modern theme of **wood** was also the traditional theme for the fifth anniversary, so you may have already used up your wooden gift ideas!

However, **calla lilies**, the associated flowers, have become popular in recent years and are readily available from florists. Their symbolism connects them with life and rebirth, as well as resurrection after death. Calla lilies are closely related to the wild British arum called Lords-and-ladies, so named because its spadix and leaves are said to resemble male and female genitalia, so life and rebirth seem more appropriate. The word calla means beauty in Greek.

Both **amethyst** and **garnet** are associated with the 6th anniversary. Although amethyst (a type of quartz) is associated with at least three different anniversary milestones, it is most strongly connected with the sixth anniversary. Amethyst is said to have healing powers for both emotional and physical conditions. It was also thought by ancient Greeks to protect the wearer from drunkenness, but I wouldn't bank on that at your anniversary celebrations!

Seventh Anniversary

⊚ Wool or copper is the traditional theme
⊚ The modern theme is a desk set

A husband or a wife is a promise that you will have a friend forever
– Author unknown

Wool was one of the most ancient fibres used in the making of clothes. It is associated with warmth and comfort. If you find it difficult to source a live sheep for your seventh anniversary gift, there is no shortage of woollen items to choose from instead.

Anything made of the alternative theme of **copper** would be fine too. Copper is a supreme conductor of energy and is said to have associated healing qualities, promoting unity, harmony and love.

The modern theme is a **desk set**. Who dreamed that up? Desk sets (often including ink wells) were common in the 19th and early 20th century. Their dip pens and ink wells are now largely replaced by rollerball pens and often include tidy trays for paper clips etc. As an inspired alternative (especially if the happy couple don't have a desk!), you could buy them the 1957 film *Desk Set*, a romantic comedy classic starring Spencer Tracy and Katherine Hepburn.

Two flowers are commonly found on the seven-year anniversary lists – **freesia** and **jack-in-the-pulpit**. Freesia symbolizes friendship and faithfulness. Jack-in-the-pulpit is a native of the US that symbolizes shelter. Its spathe represents a pulpit, whilst its central spadix is Jack, where the flower's reproductive parts are found.

The gemstones identified for the seventh anniversary are **onyx** (see also 10th anniversary) or the illustrated **lapis lazuli**, one of the stones also earmarked for the ninth anniversary. The latter is said to promote harmony in a relationship.

Eighth Anniversary

⚘ The traditional theme is bronze and, in the UK, also pottery
⚘ The modern equivalent is lace or linen

A marriage anniversary is the celebration of love, trust, partnership, tolerance and tenacity – Author unknown

This is an anniversary of overlapping themes. **Bronze** and **pottery** are both ancient materials, reflecting longevity and reliability. So no surprise that they pop up for other anniversaries too: bronze, an alloy of copper and tin, is also the primary theme for the 19th anniversary. And pottery is a theme for the ninth anniversary while porcelain is also the 18th anniversary theme and china the 20th.

Pottery is defined as an item made of baked clay, i.e. clay hardened in a kiln. Clay is usually either earthenware or stoneware, the former being fired at a lower temperature, making it softer and more easily broken. Porcelain is made from a fine, white earthenware clay of the same name. It was first produced in China, giving rise to china becoming the generic name for both porcelain and any imitation of it, i.e. almost any item of ceramic, glazed tableware. Bone china is a particular type of porcelain. Got it? So now you can plan your whole sequence of appropriate gifts!

Lace or **linen** is the modern theme, but lace is also the undisputed traditional theme for the 13th anniversary, and you may already have given linen as a fourth anniversary gift!

Clematis is the most commonly-associated flower for the eighth anniversary in many lists. It symbolises ingenuity or mental agility, due to its habit of climbing anywhere! But it also entwines as it grows….

One of the appropriate gems is the **tourmaline**. It symbolises energy and zest for life and comes in a greater range of colours than any other stone. Each colour has a different name.

Ninth Anniversary

⊛ The traditional theme in the UK is pottery or willow;
just pottery in the US
⊛ The modern theme is leather

Don't ever stop dating your wife and don't ever stop flirting with your husband – Author unknown

Pottery appears in most lists as the primary ninth theme. Its definition is already included in the preceding text.

An alternative traditional theme in the UK is **willow**, a tree with many ancient connotations. One of its features is flexibility – it bends without breaking. This quality gives rise to it being a metaphor for adaptability in both relationships and in life.

Leather is the modern theme in both the UK and the US, but has also been mentioned previously as the traditional theme of the third anniversary.

The flower which most lists associate with the ninth anniversary is the **poppy**, with the **bird of paradise flower** often getting a mention too. The poppy has been the source of opium for thousands of years, so it should be no surprise that its traditional associations were those of sleep, dreaminess, imagination and even oblivion. Poppies growing amidst the fallen on the battlefields of the two world wars, however, have given rise to their modern symbolism of remembrance and peace.

The ninth anniversary gemstone is the **tiger ey**e, which is said to promote self-confidence and dispel fear in the wearer. It was traditionally known as the 'shape-shifter' and was worn to ward off evil.

Tenth Anniversary

❦ Traditional themes are tin or aluminium
❦ Diamond is the modern gift

I saw that you were perfect, and so I loved you. Then I saw that you were not perfect and I loved you even more – Angelita Lim

Tin is one of the 'seven metals of alchemy' (along with gold, silver, mercury, copper, lead and iron). It was first mined over five thousand years ago and, when melted with copper, forms bronze. Our ancestors associated metals with spiritual qualities: tin symbolises wisdom and knowledge. In the UK, tin mining began around 2000 BC and developed over time into a prominent industry, especially in Cornwall, but it was never as significant in the US.

However, the US was a major supplier of bauxite, the ore from which **aluminium** is derived. By the early twentieth century it produced over half the world's supply, perhaps explaining why aluminium has become an additional anniversary theme in the US but not in the UK!

The modern theme for the tenth anniversary is **diamond**, but there are clearly some less expensive gift options as long as you maintain that you're just being a staunch traditionalist. A tin of beans or a canned drink will do the trick. At least you can fully justify being a cheapskate.

The tenth anniversary flower is the **daffodil**. One of the first spring flowers to appear after winter, it symbolises rebirth and regeneration. It is a member of the amaryllis family with the scientific name of Narcissus, the vain Greek god who fell in love with his own reflection in a lake and drowned himself in despair. On reflection, not a good idea.

The alternative tenth anniversary stone to diamond is **black onyx**. This is said to support mental and physical strength, to protect the wearer from harm and absorb negativity.

Eleventh Anniversary

@ **The traditional theme is steel**
@ **The modern theme is fashion jewellery**

May this marriage be full of laughter, our every day in paradise
– Rumi, Persian poet 1207-1273

Steel is iron with a very small percentage of carbon added. Like iron, steel symbolises strength and fortitude, making it a most appropriate theme to recognise the start of a couple's second decade together. Gift ideas are potentially endless, from a nail file to a private yacht (I recommend the former). Indeed, you could combine both traditional and modern anniversary themes and give a piece of steel **jewellery**. Job done!

Two flowers have become associated with the 11th anniversary: the **tulip** and the illustrated **morning glory**. The latter takes its name from its habit of flowering in the morning for just one day. This has given rise to it symbolising not only love but also mortality. So make the most of things while you can. Especially if the associated Chinese folklore around this flower resonates: two young lovers were so consumed by their love they ignored their other duties. The gods punished them by only allowing them to meet for one day a year. Gods can be tough...

Turquoise is the associated gemstone for the 11th anniversary and has been found in jewellery dating back to 4000 BC. Arizona is one of the most significant producers of this gem, which symbolises a prosperous and healthy future. An alternative stone illustrated is **haematite**. Often found in fashion jewellery, it represents self-esteem and confidence.

Twelfth Anniversary

§ **The traditional theme in the UK is silk or linen;**
silk or home décor in the US
§ **The modern theme is pearl**

Where there is love there is life
– Mahatma Gandhi, Indian politician 1869-1948

The primary theme of **silk** is common to both countries. The production of silk is stranger than fiction: the cocoon threads made by the silkworm (not a worm at all but the caterpillar of a moth) were woven first by the Chinese five thousand years ago. It is said the emperor's wife was taking tea when a cocoon from an overhanging mulberry tree fell into her cup. Rather than panic, she stared at the threads while the potential for making beautiful gowns opened up before her eyes. Silk was valuable and highly prized in ancient China, but presumably not by the countless millions of moths which are sacrificed in its production!

Only flax plants lose their life in the manufacture of **linen**, a strong cloth which is the alternative UK theme. The US alternative is **home décor**. Both give ample opportunities to purchase a related gift.

Pearl is the modern gift after 12 years together but it is also the primary theme for the 30th anniversary, where it is elaborated further.

The **peony** is the 12th anniversary's flower, symbolising romance, prosperity and honour. It is also said to be an indication of good luck and a happy marriage.

Jade and **agate** are the associated gemstones. Jade is said to be lucky and they both symbolise love and prosperity, qualities resonating with those of the peony. As the illustration implies, you could combine themes: e.g. a home décor item made of jade or agate – be creative!

Thirteenth Anniversary

㊉ **The traditional theme is lace**
㊉ **The modern theme is fur or textiles**

*Chains do not hold a marriage together. It is threads, hundreds of tiny
threads, which sew people together through the years*
– Simone Signoret, French Actress 1921-1985

Symbolising purity and innocence, **lace** is the traditional theme for the
13th anniversary. It was first made in the sixteenth century from linen
and then silk thread. Cotton was used from the nineteenth century.
I once watched an old woman in Brugge who sat flinging dozens of
bobbins, each on the end of a long thread, around a large leather pad
at an amazing speed. Every now and again she would stop and insert
a pin in a strategic point before continuing. Her seemingly random
flings were in fact being controlled with amazing precision, resulting
in exquisite hand-made lace, an incredible skill to witness. But the
Industrial Revolution brought us machines which can make increasingly
complex lace patterns. Most hand-made lace has become commercially
redundant, restricted to a luxury niche market.

The modern theme of **fur**, looking best on the stoat depicted, is said
to represent wealth and happiness. **Textiles** are a less controversial gift.

Chrysanthemum is the 13th anniversary's flower in most lists, with
the **hollyhock** appearing in some. Although chrysanthemums have some
associations with grief or mortality, they are also known as symbols of
plenty, loyalty, optimism, loveliness and happiness. Hollyhocks, on the
other hand, symbolise fertility and fruitfulness, so you might want to
know the couple's plans for the future before landing them with these!

Citrine, the gemstone of the 13th anniversary, represents well-being,
self-esteem and positivity: certainly not unlucky thirteen!

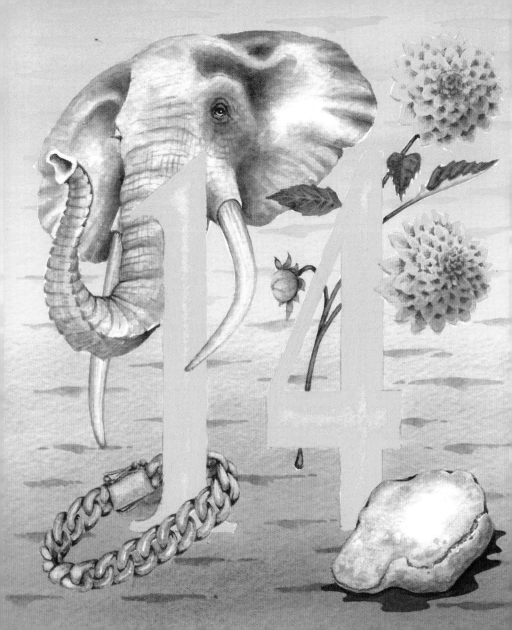

Fourteenth Anniversary

☙ Ivory is the traditional theme
☙ Gold jewellery is the modern one

Marriage is not a noun; it's a verb. It isn't something you get. It's something you do. It's the way you love your partner every day
– Barbara De Angelis, US author 1951-

From early times people have regarded **ivory** as a symbol of chastity, opulence and virtue. Consequently, it was identified as a suitable anniversary theme. Many skilfully carved artefacts have been made from ivory over the centuries (including piano keys and early snooker balls). But it is now generally accepted that ivory should remain on the creatures themselves. Ornaments of elephants are recommended in many lists as an alternative gift and this seems a viable suggestion. No country may legally trade ivory across its borders. Within the UK, ivory artefacts made before 1947 were traded until December 2018. Then a new law imposed a complete ban with just a few specific exceptions; the US adopted a similar almost total ban in July 2016.

But **gold jewellery** is the modern theme.

The flower associated with the 14th anniversary is the **dahlia**. There are many colours and varieties. They symbolise innocence and purity, or love and commitment.

Most lists name the gemstone **opal** for the 14th anniversary gift, though various alternatives also appear. Opal is said to protect the wearer from harm.

Fifteenth Anniversary

❧ The traditional theme is crystal
❧ The modern theme is a watch

*Success in marriage does not come merely through finding the right
mate, but through being the right mate*
– Barnette R. Brickner, US Rabbi 1892-1958

The traditional theme of **crystal** is also an alternative for the third anniversary. Many substances in addition to gemstones have a crystalline structure and may legitimately be termed crystals. So there is a huge range of gift ideas ranging from a simple glass tumbler to an elaborate crystal chandelier, from a few grains of salt to a two-foot tall geode of amethyst. That's crystal clear.

Watches are the modern 15th anniversary theme.

The **rose** is identified as the 15th anniversary flower in most (but not all) lists. There are about 150 wild varieties but also many hundreds of garden varieties. Early American settlers sentimentally took British roses with them but also sent back native American roses to the UK. Their many different colours all symbolise distinct meanings.

Not everyone will be familiar with the illustrated gemstone crystal **mondolite**, associated with this anniversary. It is also known as **red amethyst**, getting its colour from its haematite content. It is said to have the healing powers of amethyst but also the ability to lend courage and energy to the wearer. Other stones such as **rhodolite** (a type of garnet) are also associated with the 15th anniversary.

Sixteenth Anniversary

⚙ **Tungsten or silver is the traditional UK theme;
there is none for the US**
⚙ **The modern theme in both the UK and US is
silver holloware or coffee**

I want to remember every minute, always, always to the end of my days
– Celia Johnson, *Brief Encounter*

After the 15th anniversary, some lists only identify every fifth year, some every tenth and some only particularly significant anniversaries such as silver, ruby or gold (this is particularly true for traditional lists). Thus there is no traditional 16th anniversary theme listed for the US even though the UK has two: **tungsten** and **silver**. Silver is not only a traditional theme for both this and the 25th anniversary, it also features in the 5th and 23rd. For the 16th modern theme it becomes specifically silver holloware, i.e. bowls, dishes or anything hollow.

But a number of lists also recommend the modern alternative of **coffee**, said to symbolise the emotions and friendship.

The **aster**, so-called talisman of love, is the flower for the 16th anniversary but is also sometimes linked to the 20th. It is said to symbolise patience and elegance but was also thought to be enchanted, its petals when burned warding off evil spirits. There are many varieties, including the illustrated **michaelmas daisy**.

The **peridot** (also pictured) is identified as this anniversary's gemstone and is a symbol of love.

Seventeenth Anniversary

A good marriage is like a casserole – only those responsible for it really know what goes in it – Author unknown

No traditional theme is defined for this anniversary. And **furniture** is a gift which perhaps needs some consultation before you buy...

So the easier gift might well be **red carnations**, which are the associated blooms. The carnation is also the flower related to the first anniversary. Red carnations, should you choose that colour, are said to symbolise admiration, love and affection. But there is a further distinction: light red carnations best represent admiration and dark red carnations symbolise love and affection. Don't mess up! Perhaps you should get a combination of the two shades to be on the safe side.

Two gemstones are associated with the 17th anniversary: **pink tourmaline** and the **carnelian**. The former represents love, joy, happiness and humanity. It is thought to help healers empathise with their patient or client and enhance their healing powers. Carnelian was called 'the setting sun' by the Egyptians and more recently 'the singer's stone' because of its reputed quality of giving confidence to the wearer. Other qualities which carnelian is said to promote include motivation, endurance, leadership, courage and energy, as well as a sense of humour – often needed in a good partnership!

Eighteenth Anniversary

@ **No traditional theme identified**
@ **The modern theme is porcelain or appliances**

A successful marriage requires falling in love many times, always with the same person – Mignon McLaughlin, US author 1913-1983

Although life expectancy was lower in the past, so were divorce rates. Significantly too, people married at a younger age and so one would think that being married for eighteen years was fairly common. But there was no traditional gift associated with the anniversary. American National Retail Jewelers Association to the rescue! In 1937 it established its more comprehensive list, with **porcelain** for the 18th anniversary.

Others anniversary list-makers then chipped in, wanting to add more useful items. So the modern alternative of **appliances** came along. It could mean anything! A nice gleaming new chainsaw comes under that definition, as does a simple toaster. The choice is yours: an appliance is not the most romantic of gifts but it can tick the box.

The **cat's eye** is the 18th anniversary gemstone. **Aquamarine** is listed as an alternative, though this is also a stone for the 19th. A cat's eye is a gem with a line of light going across the centre caused by mineral fibres. It is found most commonly in the gemstone **chrysoberyl** and symbolises positive energy.

Blue is the colour associated with the 18th anniversary, so it would be reasonable to choose any **blue flowers**. The illustration is of cornflowers, also known as bachelor's button, which have long been associated with romance. Traditionally, if a young man wore a cornflower and it faded quickly, it was a sign that his love was not returned…

Nineteenth Anniversary

๑ **The traditional theme in the UK is furniture**
๑ **The modern theme in UK and US is bronze**

Journeys end in lovers' meeting – William Shakespeare, *Twelfth Night*

Both **furniture** and **bronze** are themes which have appeared earlier in the anniversary chronology: furniture for the 17th and bronze for the 8th. Garden furniture or furniture-related ornaments provide variation if the traditional theme is being considered as a gift idea. But bronze also provides options.

Bronze is made from elements of the earth – copper and tin, so has associations with nature. It reflects a down-to-earth attitude and a humble nature. It also symbolises strength and stability. Many seemingly bronze artefacts these days are in fact manufactured from spelter, a cheaper alloy consisting mainly of zinc. While perhaps not for the purist, it provides a more affordable alternative to the real thing.

In the absence of any specific flower associated with this anniversary, included in a number of lists is a bronze-leaved plant, of which there are many, including the **bronze dahlia** variety illustrated.

A number of gemstones are named for the 19th anniversary. The **topaz** in the illustration comes in a variety of other colours and is also the preferred stone for the fourth anniversary. The ancient Greeks thought it increased and protected physical and mental strength, while the ancient Egyptians associated yellow topaz with the sun god Ra and thought it bestowed his protection upon them. Other listed gems include **aquamarine** and **golden beryl**.

Twentieth Anniversary

🕭 **China is the traditional theme**
🕭 **China or platinum is the modern one**

*Never marry the one you can live with, marry the one you cannot
live without* – Author unknown

Today, the term **china** is essentially used to refer to any ceramic
object, particularly glazed tableware. Originally it referred to Chinese
porcelain, then to imitations of that porcelain, and subsequently to
almost anything made of fired clay. In one sense, the clay from which
china is made includes three of the four natural elements which are part
of the next three anniversary themes. Clay is very much of the earth
(one could say it is earth itself), it contains water which makes it soft and
malleable, and becomes hardened ceramic by the heat from fire.

Platinum is an alternative modern theme. However, it is also the
sole theme for the 70th anniversary, where it is explored in greater detail.
Similarly, the **emerald** as this anniversary's gemstone is explained fully
in the 55th anniversary, when it is the primary theme. It is also listed
for 35th.

Most lists identify the illustrated **daylily** or the **aster** (see also 16th)
as the flower for this anniversary. Daylilies are so called because a flower
opens in the morning and lasts just 24 hours. Whilst 'true' lilies symbolise
purity and devotion, daylilies are associated with motherhood. The plant
is widely eaten in China. It is said to have a number of health benefits
including helping to get to sleep.

Twenty-First Anniversary

- There is no US traditional theme; in the UK it is brass
- A fire theme and brass or nickel appear in modern lists

There is no more lovely, friendly, and charming relationship,
communion or company than a good marriage
– Martin Luther, German theologian 1483-1546

Some lists identify the four natural elements of fire, water, air and stone (earth) for anniversaries 21 to 24. These were the essence of all things according to a number of ancient cultures, though they have been added to over the centuries.

An alloy of copper and zinc, **brass** is said to encourage good health and develop the immune system. Many household objects and ornaments, as well as the traditional working horse brasses pictured, were made from this material, offering wide choice for a gift.

Another modern alternative is **nickel**, a shiny, silvery-white metal. Though it has many uses, it is perhaps most associated with the US five cent piece (now there's a gift idea!). The coin was originally made of silver and only became the 'nickel' in the mid nineteenth century.

There are no specific flowers linked to the 21st anniversary. However, orange is an associated colour, so the illustrated **bird of paradise plant**, also known as the **crane flower**, might be worth considering. It is said to symbolise magnificence and splendour, as well as faithfulness.

The illustration also shows **iolite**, the stone for this anniversary. Occurring in deep shades of blue to violet, it was called the Vikings' Compass, reflecting its use by them to use the sun as an aid to navigation. It has consequent associations with journeying, exploration, motivation and confidence.

Twenty-Second Anniversary

In the UK the traditional theme is copper
Water and copper are modern themes in UK and US

If I had a flower for every time I thought of you, I could walk through my garden forever – Alfred Lord Tennyson, English poet 1809-1892

Copper is not only the traditional UK theme for the 22nd anniversary, it is also the modern one in the UK and US. It is shown submerged and naturally oxidising in this illustration. Oxidised copper or verdigris is beautiful in its own right; it is often created for outdoor artefacts and has been used as a pigment for paintings. Copper is highly conductive and so used for electrical cables. That ability to transport energy gives rise to its stated healing qualities: helping circulation, increasing vitality and oxygen levels, repairing tissue etc. Copper bracelets have long been worn as a particular help in combating arthritis, though this has been questioned by recent studies.

Water, associated with this anniversary, is one of the four original 'natural elements' and often represents life itself. Life on earth began in the seas and we cannot live without it. So what couple wouldn't want a water jug or tumblers as an anniversary gift! The fish illustrated is a green tench, reflecting this anniversary's associated colour.

Many lists feature **spinel** (pictured) as the gemstone for the 22nd anniversary. It can be found in different colours and is said to represent hope and optimism, vitality and joie de vivre.

Twenty-Third Anniversary

⚜ The traditional theme in the UK is silver plate
⚜ An air theme and silver plate appear in modern lists

You know you're in love when you can't fall asleep because reality is finally better than your dreams – Dr Seuss, author, 1904-1991

Air, like water, is essential for life and is one of the original four natural elements. Its modern association with the 23rd anniversary is identified in just a few lists. A hot air balloon trip? A flight to somewhere exotic?

Silver plate is more widely recognised as the theme. It is sometimes known as Sheffield plate after the English city where it was invented in the mid 18th century. A thin coating of silver is fused onto a base of cheaper metal, usually copper, to produce the effect of solid silver more economically. Over time, the coating can get worn away.

Silver itself is particularly associated with the 25th anniversary but also with the 5th and 16th. It is a precious metal and as such has associations with wealth and prosperity. It can be wrought into ornate shapes and is considered an elegant material. Silver plate gave the opportunity for more people to own things which at least appeared to be made of this sophisticated material. A silver-plate plate is illustrated!

Imperial topaz is the very specific associated gemstone identified within many lists, with an alternative being **sapphire** (see also 45th and 65th). Topaz occurs naturally in a number of colours, but stones are also artificially treated to create more. Orange-yellow or golden topaz is referred to as imperial. It is a stone of good fortune, bringing success and prosperity to the wearer (see also fourth).

There is no 23rd anniversary flower identified.

Twenty-Fourth Anniversary

🎵 The traditional theme in the US is opal
🎵 Modern lists show a stone theme or musical instruments

*People are like musical instruments: their sound depends
on who touches them* – Virgil, Roman poet 70BC-19BC

Although most lists show no traditional themes at all for the 24th anniversary, just a few do identify **opal** for the US. This appears to be the only anniversary where a traditional theme is seen for the US while the UK has none. Opal is also associated with the 14th anniversary; in addition to protection from harm, it is said to encourage independence and creativity.

The fourth natural element is earth, but this is listed as **stone** in the few modern lists. Earth and stone symbolise strength, endurance and permanence, also practicality and being 'down to earth'.

Musical instruments were identified as the other modern theme in the US jewellers' association list of 1937. The ability of music to stir the emotions, whether to evoke fierce passion or to soothe and calm, should resonate with the range of experiences over 24 years of marriage. And there are many forms in which music could manifest itself as a gift.

The illustrated **tanzanite** is this anniversary's gemstone. As the stone was only discovered in 1967 (reputedly by Maasai cattle-herders), it is clearly a recent addition to the anniversary inventories and an indication of how these can change and evolve. Tanzanite is too new for there to be any associated folklore.

Although no flower is listed for the 24th anniversary, the associated colour is **lavender**. So there's no reason why this shrub shouldn't be the perfect solution!

Twenty-Fifth Anniversary

⊚ **Silver is the traditional theme**
⊚ **The modern theme is sterling silver**

*Value love more than anything else... it will outlast all the gold
and silver of the earth* – Author unknown

The theme of **silver** is universally agreed across every published list, probably because it reflects one of the oldest traditions. Along with gold for the 50th anniversary, it was established long before other anniversary themes were even considered. It is quite an achievement to reach a silver wedding anniversary and sadly only a minority of married couples manage it.

Silver is associated with the moon and with the feminine; it is said to reflect back the energy someone gives out, whether that be positive or negative. Silver or 'fine silver' is 99.9% pure silver, whilst sterling silver is just 92.5% pure. The lower value modern theme suggests that expectations (or standards) have slipped over the years, but if you don't want second best, there's still a wide variety of affordable fine silver objects which could be considered.

Equally well, the silver theme can be applied to other things – plants with **silver foliage**, for example. Or there's a rose variety called Silver Lining and another called Silver Shadows. Or of course you could buy a white mouse for the grateful couple and name it Silver...

A number of lists associate the **iris** with the 25th anniversary. In Greek mythology, Iris was the goddess of the rainbow, but the flower's symbolism includes wisdom and trust. Regarded as a 'royal' flower and inspiring the fleur-de-lis, it also has associations with elegance and sophistication.

Thirtieth Anniversary

⊗ **The traditional theme is pearl**
⊗ **The modern theme is pearl or diamond**

If I get married, I want to be very married
– Audrey Hepburn, British actress 1929-1993

Pearls certainly have the shining beauty to symbolise thirty years of being together. They are unique among precious stones in that they need no cutting or polishing, and they come from rivers or the sea rather than the depths of the earth. The freshwater pearl features for the first anniversary so it seems reasonable that the 30th anniversary's gem should be the **saltwater pearl**. They are naturally formed when a foreign body gets into the shell. The host (usually an oyster) defends itself by producing a layer of fluid to cover the irritant. After multiple layers are built up, the pearl is formed. Cultured pearls are made when farmed molluscs have a prepared nucleus inserted into them in order that they continue to build up the layers of fluid to form a pearl. Pearls are said to attract wealth, bring luck, offer protection, impose calm, strengthen relationships, and keep the wearer safe. What pearls of wisdom!

The modern alternative is a **diamond**, also associated with 10th, 60th and 75th anniversary.

Two flowers are identified for the 30th anniversary – **amaryllis lily** and **sweet pea**. The former blooms for a lengthy time, reflecting the longevity of the relationship and symbolising strength and pride. Although sweet peas represent pleasure, they are also associated with parting and farewells, albeit after an enjoyable time. It may not be quite the message you want to convey…!

Thirty-Fifth Anniversary

⊗ Coral is the traditional theme
⊗ The modern theme is jade

A happy marriage is a long conversation which always seems too short
– André Maurois, French author 1885-1967

Coral, like a relationship, is a living, vibrant thing. A branch of coral is made up of thousands of organisms called polyps. Coral polyps are actually invertebrates, usually tiny but sometimes growing to the size of the mushroom polyp at over five inches. They can take many forms but together create one of the most diverse ecosystems on earth – the coral reef – supporting a quarter of all marine species. This habitat is challenged by climate change and the associated problem of the ocean becoming more acidic. Many coral reefs have become bleached and have subsequently died. Consequently, this wonderful natural resource requires protection and conservation. Like fur, ivory and other products derived from living wild creatures, its harvesting is increasingly controversial. Coral is said to possess sacred qualities. Red coral has been particularly prized. Because of its colour, it is associated with Mars. Its symbolism includes wealth and health, but also wisdom, happiness and immortality.

Jade is therefore probably the better choice of gift. It is both the modern theme everywhere as well as a traditional theme in the US. It is also associated with the 12th anniversary. To the qualities of jade already outlined there, can be added the symbolism of purity and peace. **Emerald** is named in many lists as the 35th anniversary's stone. It is also the primary theme for the 55th anniversary, where there is further information.

There is no associated flower.

Fortieth Anniversary

ꙮ The traditional and modern theme is ruby

He felt now that he was not simply close to her, but that he did not know where he ended and she began – Leo Tolstoy, *Anna Karenina*

There is unequivocal agreement about the theme for the 40th anniversary – **ruby**. Sometimes poetically described as a 'drop of earth's blood', the ruby is a rare gem, with large rubies over three carats far more scarce than large diamonds. Rubies come primarily from India and Burma, the latter often producing the better-quality stones. Rubies share much of their symbolism with that of their colour red – love, passion, desire, sensuality, longing, lust. It is certainly seen as a fiercely romantic stone. But it is also said to have a whole range of health attributes, including detoxifying the body and preventing and curing disease. It was even thought to restore youth when rubbed on the skin. You wish…

Relatively few lists identify a flower for the 40th anniversary. Those that do don't always agree. Some suggest **nasturtium**, whilst others define the illustrated **gladiolus**. This flower can symbolise strength and moral integrity but also passion, the latter particularly apt for the Ruby celebrations. The other flower illustrated is the 'Ruby Wedding', a specific variety of **rose** appropriate as a 40th anniversary gift if rubies aren't an option!

There are a number of creatures with ruby in their name, such as the illustrated Ruby Tiger moth. Others include the Ruby-throated Hummingbird, the Ruby-tailed Wasp, the Ruby-cheeked Sunbird, the Ruby-crowned Kinglet… I could go on.

Forty-Fifth Anniversary

⊛ The traditional and modern theme is sapphire

Our wedding was many years ago. The celebration continues to this day
– Gene Perret, US screenwriter and author 1937-

Claims are sometimes made of anniversary lists that themes for the earlier years are for more practical, useful items, while the themes as the years progress represent more valuable items. There are certainly examples of where this is the case and the much later anniversaries do often include valuable gems.

Two anniversaries have **sapphires** as a dominant theme – this and the 65th anniversary's star sapphire. Sapphires come in many colours except red: red sapphires are actually rubies! They are all made from the same material. However, sapphires are typically blue and this colour is the most sought after. Blue sapphires symbolise the heavens and are said to have a multitude of properties including the ability to bestow health, wisdom, safety, faith, happiness and prosperity.

There is no additional gemstone or flower associated with this anniversary.

Fiftieth Anniversary

⚜ Gold is both the traditional and modern theme

Love is the only gold – Alfred Lord Tennyson, English poet 1809-1892

Gold, gold and more gold! Being one of the oldest anniversary traditions, there is complete agreement about the theme for the 50th anniversary. Together with the Silver 25th, this anniversary was recognised long before other themes were suggested.

Gold represents triumph, achievement and success. A gold medal award is the highest possible commendation, so gold is the appropriate recognition for fifty years of togetherness. It is likely that a couple initially cemented their relationship with a gold ring. The colour gold is said to symbolise wisdom and enlightenment, so the gold from that ring also represents the deep understanding of a person's inner self and soul, as well as that of their partner fifty years on.

Gold is also a symbol of wealth and prosperity. Many metaphors reflect it: a successful enterprise might be a 'gold mine' or the 'goose that lays the golden egg', the entrepreneur having a 'golden touch'. An idea might have 'struck gold', a time of success might be a 'golden age'. If you're off to the couple's celebrations, be 'as good as gold'!

Two flowers are associated with the 50th anniversary: **yellow roses** and **violets**. The former represents joy, happiness and delight, as does its sunshine colour. Violets symbolise humility and faithfulness, a necessary quality for fifty years of devotion. It was a flower used in love potions and was considered a symbol of fertility and love by the ancient Greeks.

Fifty-Fifth Anniversary

⊛ **The traditional and modern theme is emerald**

*Love is a fruit in season at all times and within the reach of every hand.
Anyone may gather it and no limit is set* – Mother Teresa 1910-97

In the 21st century, roughly only a third of married couples reach their 25th anniversary. Around a fifth reach their 35th anniversary but only 5% reach their 50th anniversary. Beyond that the numbers are even lower – so what an achievement it is to get to the 55th!

Emerald is also associated with the 20th and the 35th anniversary, but the stone has suffered from some controversy. A number of different gems, including aquamarine, morganite and emeralds themselves are all made from the same mineral – beryl. Beryl becomes green when chrome or vanadium is present within it. Traditionally, only those stones coloured by chrome were considered to be true emeralds. In the 1960s, American jewellers included beryl containing vanadium in that elite category, but this has not been universally accepted. A further controversy concerns an extremely rare stone found in Utah with a very similar chemical composition to green emerald – red beryl. So is it a red-coloured emerald? The jury is undecided on that too!

The gemstone gives its name to the colour emerald green, of course, inspiring the names of the illustrated Emerald Tree Boa and the Emerald moth. But if you want to give a brilliant green gift, something from the Emerald Isle of Ireland might inspire you.

Some lists identify the **calla lily** for the 55th anniversary. With symbolism of both life and renewal of life, it is also linked to the sixth.

Sixtieth Anniversary

◎ Diamond is the traditional and modern theme

Diamonds are a girl's best friend and dogs are a man's best friend.
Now you know which of the sexes has more sense
– Zsa Zsa Gabor, Hungarian/American actress 1917-2016

Considered by the ancient Greeks to be tears of the Gods, **diamonds** have been on the earth for billions of years, as timeless as the couple who have managed to stay together for sixty of them! They are said not only to reflect light, but to symbolise the sun's light and indeed life itself. They are emblems of brilliance and purity and signify the enduring commitment of a couple to their relationship.

The word diamond derives from the Greek word *adamas*, meaning invincible. It is the hardest material on earth, with remarkable resistance to scratching. A diamond's quality is usually judged by the four Cs – Carat, Clarity, Colour and Cut. Carat is simply the weight, and clarity how clear or transparent the stone is. Perhaps surprisingly, diamonds come in all colours of the spectrum, with the most colourless being the rarest and most valuable. When they come out of the ground, diamonds are dull; it is only when cut and polished that they sparkle. They can be cut in different ways to maximise their brilliance or how they reflect light. Such cuts can be an indication of a piece of jewellery's age, as different cuts evolved over time. Diamond is so hard that it wasn't until the thirteenth century that people found out how to cut them to improve their optical impact.

Diamonds are also associated the 10th, 30th, the 75th and each subsequent anniversary beyond. There is no flower or alternative gemstone identified.

Sixty-Fifth Anniversary

✆ The traditional and modern theme is Star Sapphire

As we grow older together, as we continue to change with age, there is one thing that will never change ... I will always keep falling in love with you — Karen Clodfelder

Whilst sapphire is also associated with the 45th, the 65th anniversary's theme is specifically **star sapphir**e. This is a rare gemstone which contains inclusions, structured in such a way that it produces a six-rayed star across its surface when viewed in certain light conditions. To maximise the effect, they are usually polished in a cabochon or rounded form. Because of their blue colour, star sapphires are symbols of the sky. They are also reputed to imbue wisdom, love and devotion, so a star sapphire would appear to be the ideal theme for such a significant anniversary.

Sapphire is also within the given name of many different creatures around the globe. One of the most interesting is the illustrated Sea Sapphire, a tiny marine crustacean which pulses spectacularly with iridescent blue light. Other creatures pictured are the Sapphire Flycatcher, the Sapphire-tailed Clearwing (a wasp-impersonating moth) and the Powdery Green Sapphire butterfly (which is a member of the blues family of butterflies and is actually blue!)

There is no flower or alternative gemstone associated with this anniversary.

Seventieth Anniversary

Platinum is the traditional and modern theme

Our anniversary is just a momentary celebration,
but our marriage is a timeless one – Author unknown

Both the traditional and modern theme for the 70th anniversary is platinum. **Platinum** is a silvery-white precious metal and symbolises strength, purity and love. As one of the least reactive, non-brittle metals, it does not corrode and can be drawn into thin strands, so lends itself ideally to jewellery manufacture. Such jewellery represents love's eternal charm and endurance, making platinum a most appropriate gift theme to celebrate seventy years of being together.

Perhaps the most famous couple to have celebrated their platinum wedding anniversary is Queen Elizabeth II and Prince Philip. They were married in 1947 at Westminster Abbey and so celebrated their platinum anniversary in 2017. Quite an achievement! But the record length for a royal marriage is held by Prince and Princess Mikasa of Japan, who married in 1941. At the Prince's death in 2016, aged 100, they had been married for 75 years.

Platinum is a scarce metal and therefore valuable. It has a number of uses in addition to making jewellery, especially as a catalyst to influence various chemical reactions. One of these is within a vehicle's catalytic converter, a component which renders toxic compounds from the exhaust less harmful. Platinum's inclusion has led to a modern spate in thefts of catalytic converters from cars, in order to melt down the platinum.

This anniversary does not have any flower or gemstone associated with it.

Seventy-Fifth Anniversary

☙ The traditional and modern theme is diamond or gold

You should be kissed and often, and by someone who knows how
– Rhett Butler in *Gone With The Wind*

In the late nineteenth century, as anniversary lists were growing in popularity, the **diamond** was increasingly recognised as the symbol for the 75th anniversary. Queen Victoria's 60 years on the throne were widely celebrated as her 'Diamond' Jubilee, so the 60th became the anniversary most closely associated with this gem.

So many qualities are attributed to the diamond. One of them is the ability to instil love and faithfulness, so it is easy to see how diamonds have been associated with many different anniversaries. But not everyone will have the means to buy a diamond as a gift and although gold is an alternative theme, there is no further gemstone associated with this anniversary.

Neither is there any association of a specific flower. However, there is a **rose** called The Diamond Wedding as well as one called Diamond Jubilee. Or what about a Neil Diamond record? Or a pack of cards with lots of diamonds in it!

The anniversary shares its diamond theme with 10th, 30th and each milestone at five-year intervals from 80th to 100th. Its alternative is **gold** which it shares with the 14th and 50th anniversaries. The 50th anniversary entry describes in greater detail gold's symbolism and qualities.

The illustration shows two creatures of the many that have diamond included in their names. The Diamond Dove is a type of Australian pigeon; the Diamond-backed Terrapin lives in southern and eastern states of America. Both are sometimes kept as pets.

Eightieth Anniversary

❦ **Oak is the traditional theme in the UK**
❦ **The modern theme in US and UK is diamond or pearl**

Love is patient, love is kind. It does not envy, it does not boast, it is not proud. It is not rude, it is not self-seeking, it is not easily angered, it keeps no record of wrongs – Corinthians 13:4-5

Although most people are likely to have their own clear picture of what an **oak** is, there are about six hundred species around the world. The term applies to the wood as well as the tree itself, of course. It has long had a special place in hearts and minds, in culture, folklore and history. It is a symbol of strength and resilience, qualities to which people often aspire. It was the symbol of Zeus in Greek mythology and is also associated with wisdom. An oak tree supports a myriad of other insects, plants and animals. The oak can live for over a thousand years, and that longevity makes it an apt symbol for an eighty-year relationship.

Although the modern themes for this anniversary are **diamond** and **pearl**, these have their own separate associations – the 60th and 30th respectively. There is surely an argument for the oak to show its resilience, hold its own and become the 80th's exclusive and universal theme – mighty oaks from little acorns grow!

There is a wide range of gift options for the theme of oak: an oak ornament, a more practical bread board, an oak-carved letter opener… Or what a beautiful gesture to plant a sapling oak tree to mark 80 happy years together, for a future generation to enjoy.

Eighty-Fifth Anniversary

**❦ Traditional themes are wine in the UK
and moonstone in the US
❦ The modern equivalent is diamond or sapphire**

Age cannot wither her, nor custom stale / Her infinite variety
– William Shakespeare, Antony and Cleopatra

Well, you certainly deserve a glass of **wine** if you've reached this anniversary. After 85 years you might even want something stronger! At the time of writing, only six couples are recognised by the Guinness World Record list to have ever made it, though a further two are not recognised but documented elsewhere. Although wine can be a symbol of transformation (as the grape is transformed through fermentation), it is also a symbol of joy and happiness, hopefully reflecting the couple's time together! Wine is thought to have been first produced over eight thousand years ago. That batch should be well ready to drink by now. Wine is an easy gift to give.

Moonstone, also known as hecatolite, is listed as the traditional theme in the US. It is a form of feldspar and has an opalescent, milky appearance. Moonstone is associated with the feminine, following the moon's orbit cycle around the earth. Its symbolism includes personal growth, emotional strength and being lucky in love.

One can see why jewellers might have decided upon the modern (expensive) themes of **diamond** or **sapphire**. As already stated, diamond is included for each of the anniversaries after 75, and the illustrated sapphire has associations also with the 45th and 65th anniversaries.

There is no associated flower.

Ninetieth Anniversary

*Love doesn't make the world go round; love is what makes the ride
worthwhile* – Franklin Jones, American journalist 1908-1980

Granite, **stone** or **marble** indeed – a couple would have to be as solid as
a rock to achieve a 90th anniversary milestone.

Just one couple are reported to have managed it so far, making it the
world's longest-ever marriage. They are said to have married in India in
1925 and subsequently moved to the UK, where in 2015 (at 110 and 103
years old respectively – a combined total of 213 years!) they celebrated
ninety years together. However, this is not recognised by the Guinness
World Record list at the time of writing: it identifies instead an American
couple as having the longest marriage. In 2008 they had been married
for 84 years, with one of the couple passing away shortly afterwards.
This record has not been surpassed officially.

Firmness and unyielding solidarity are qualities of granite and
marble. Granite has been revered and considered to have magical
qualities by different peoples around the world. It is said to encourage
positivity, while marble is said to support self-control, calm and inner
balance. Both materials are used to create artefacts and ornaments of
great beauty and reverence; many statues and monuments are made
from these two materials. Strength and beauty combined must surely be
features within any relationship of such longevity!

There is no flower or gemstone associated with this anniversary.

Ninety-Fifth Anniversary

℘ There is no traditional theme identified
℘ The modern one is ruby or diamond

I wish I had done everything on earth with you
– The Great Gatsby, Scott Fitzgerald 1896-1940

Rubies and **diamonds** have been earlier anniversary themes. They appear here for the 95th again as modern suggestions in the absence of any tradition, but we are in untrodden anniversary territory now; no couple has ever had cause to invoke their use to celebrate this anniversary and consequently, of course, no couple has ever reached the next.

In the UK, information about marriages is collected by the Office for National Statistics; in America by the US Census Bureau. Whilst there is no great assimilation of data between the two organisations, both agree that the average age of people getting married is rising, as is the percentage of people choosing to live alone and the number of couples who decide not to marry at all. The average length of a marriage is reported to be about eleven years, with 40-50% ending in divorce (though this latter figure is thought to be decreasing).

But couples do not need to be married to celebrate their increasing years together through the anniversary milestones. So whilst the data for marriages themselves may not be the most encouraging, let's hope that the prospects for couples of any status to celebrate these later anniversaries are more positive!

There is no flower or separate gemstone identified for this anniversary.

ħundredth Anniversary

⚘ **There is no traditional theme identified**
⚘ **The modern theme is 10 carat diamond**

If you live to be a hundred, I want to live to be a hundred minus one day so I never have to live without you – A.A. Milne, English author 1882-1956

Who but an association of jewellers would decide that an appropriate anniversary gift was a **10 carat diamond**! We would no doubt all admire the achievement of even living for 100 years, let alone being together as a couple for that long. But you'd need extremely deep pockets to buy the recommended theme gift. At the time of writing, the cheapest, low quality diamond of that size would set you back in the region of £138,000, or $170,000. And you may not even be able to find one for sale. Diamonds weighing 10 carats or more are extremely rare (the average size of a mined diamond is usually between 0.5 and 2 carats). So that seems to be a reasonable excuse – 'I'm so sorry! We couldn't source a 10 carat diamond anywhere, so I got you this teen-weeny little diamond chip instead.'

Of course, you're unlikely to ever need to use this line, as no couple has ever reached this incredible milestone. However, as we humans increase our life expectancy there just may be a growing demand in the future for that 10 carat stone!

Diamond is also associated with 10th, 30th, 75th and each successive five-year anniversary up to this, except for the 90th.

No flower or alternative stone is associated with the 100th anniversary.

Anniversary gifts associated with the years

Year	UK Traditional	US Traditional	UK & US Modern	Gemstone	Flower
1	paper	paper	clocks	freshwater pearl/mother of pearl	carnation
2	cotton	cotton	china	garnet/rose quartz	cosmos/lily of the valley
3	leather	leather	crystal/glass	moonstone/crystal/jade/pearl	fuchsia/sunflower
4	fruit & flowers/linen/silk	linen/silk/fruit & flowers	appliances	amethyst/blue topaz	geranium/hydrangea
5	wood	wood	silver	pink tourmaline/sapphire/turquoise	daisy
6	sugar	candy/iron	wood	amethyst/garnet	calla lily
7	wool/copper	wool/copper	desk sets	onyx/lapis lazuli	jack-in-the-pulpit
8	bronze/pottery/salt	bronze	lace/linen	tourmaline/aventurine	clematis/lilac
9	pottery/willow/copper	pottery/willow	leather	lapis lazuli/tiger-eye	poppy/bird of paradise plant
10	tin	tin/aluminium	diamond	black onyx/crystal/green tourmaline	daffodil

Year	UK Traditional	US Traditional	UK & US Modern	Gemstone	Flower
11	steel	steel	fashion jewellery	turquoise/ haematite	morning glory/ tulip
12	silk/linen	silk/home décor	pearl	jade/agate	peony
13	lace	lace	fur/textiles	citrine/ malachite/ moonstone	chrysanthemum
14	ivory	ivory/agate	gold jewellery	opal/gold/ moss agate	dahlia
15	crystal	crystal	watches	mondolite/ ruby/ alexandrite	rose
16	tungsten/ silver	none	silver holloware/ coffee	peridot/ aquamarine	aster
17	none	none	furniture/ watches	pink tourmaline/ citrine/ carnelian/ amethyst	carnation
18	none	none	porcelain/ appliances	aquamarine/ cat's eye/ tiger eye	none (blue)
19	furniture	none	bronze	topaz/ aquamarine/ golden beryl	none (bronze)

Year	UK Traditional	US Traditional	UK & US Modern	Gemstone	Flower
20	china	china	china/platinum	emerald/platinum	daylily/aster
21	brass	none	fire/brass/nickel	iolite	none (orange)
22	copper	none	water/copper	spinel/zircon	none (green)
23	silver plate	none	air/silver plate	imperial topaz	none (silver)
24	none	opal	stone/musical instruments	tanzanite	none (lavender)
25	silver	silver	sterling silver	silver/tsavorite	iris
30	pearl	pearl	pearl/diamond	pearl/diamond/jade	amaryllis lily/sweet pea
35	coral	coral/jade	jade	jade/coral/emerald	none
40	ruby	ruby	ruby	ruby	nasturtium/gladiolus
45	sapphire	sapphire	sapphire	sapphire/alexandrite	none
50	gold	gold	gold	gold	yellow rose/violet
55	emerald	emerald	emerald/turquoise	emerald/alexandrite	calla lily

Year	UK Traditional	US Traditional	UK & US Modern	Gemstone	Flower
60	diamond	yellow diamond	diamond	diamond/ emerald	none
65	star sapphire	star sapphire	star sapphire	star sapphire/ diamond	none
70	platinum	platinum	platinum	platinum	none
75	diamond/ gold	diamond/ gold	diamond/ gold	diamond/ gold	none
80	oak	none	diamond/ pearl	diamond/ pearl	none
85	wine	moonstone	diamond/ sapphire	diamond/ sapphire	none
90	granite/ stone	none	granite/ engraved marble	none	none
95	none	none	ruby/ diamond	ruby/ diamond	none
100	none	none	10 carat diamond	10 carat diamond	none

There are many anniversary gift lists. The above table features the most commonly agreed ones. There are others which are not listed here – some obscure, others specific to a particular country.

Intermediate anniversary dates

Few lists identify themes for the 'in-between' anniversaries (which are not featured in this book). Some gifts in this category are rather incongruous – a car for 32 years but groceries for 44. And how well would plastic be received after 53 years together!

26	original art or painting		43	entertainment or travel
27	music or sculpture		44	electronics, literature or groceries
28	linen or orchids		46	games or original poetry tribute
29	tools or furniture			
31	travel or timepieces		47	garden or plants or books
32	bronze, cars or conveyances		48	home improvement or optical goods
33	iron or amethyst		49	copper or any luxury item
34	food or opal			
36	antiques or bone china		51	photographs or cameras
37	books or alabaster		52	baths or spa
38	beryl, tourmaline or luck		53	plastic
			54	glass
39	lace or laughter		56	day
41	office and desk décor or land		57	night
42	clocks and watches or improved real estate		58	faith and hope
			59	charity

Notes & Reminders

....

....

....

....

....

....

....

....

....

....

....

....

....

....

Notes & Reminders

Other gift books published by Merlin Unwin Books

A Murmuration of Starlings
The Collective Nouns of Animals and Birds
Steve Palin

Wild Flowers of Britain
Month by Month
Margaret Wilson

The Pocket Guide to Essential Knots
Peter Owen

Horse Racing Terms
an illustrated guide
Rosemary Coates

Training your Puppy
Fiona Baird

www.merlinunwin.co.uk

For more about the author's work

www.theanniversarybook.co.uk
www.theanniversarybook.com